Nicholas Woo 著

そのまま使える
ネイティブ表現
800

英語でSNSトーク

はじめに

　私たち Ginko Labo では、この本の制作にあたり、意欲と、情熱を注いで、概要とテキストを仕上げました。この本を読者のみなさんが選んでくださったことをとても嬉しく思います。
　ライン、ツイッター、フェイスブック、スカイプなどで友だちと話すとき、日本語で書いた文を見て「英語にするとどうなるんだろう？」と思ったことはありませんか？そういう疑問を持っているのはすばらしいことだと思います。言葉の勉強は普段の生活からした方が一番良く、英語を自分のものにするための大事な心がけです。

　ただ、言葉は文法・単語だけでなく文化やその時の流行りなども含まれます。日本で使う決まり文句が英語にない時や、逆に日本語にないのに英語では表現されることもあります。また、日本語には漢字があるので一文字や単語で書けるものが、英語になると説明文になり長くなることもあります。また、文学ではなく普段のネイティブのおしゃべりで使われる言葉が知りたいとなると、辞書や教科書だけではわからないことが多いと思います。

　ネイティブが使っているリアルな表現が知りたい、そのニュアンスも知りたいと思ったら、この本で一緒に実際の人たちのチャットを少しのぞいて見ましょう！

　この本が、読者のみなさんの英語の習得、そして、熟達に寄与することを心から願っております。

　　　　　　　　感謝とともに
　　　　　　　　Nicholas Woo と Ginko Labo のメンバーより

To our readers

Thank you for choosing Sneak Peak. We at Ginko Labo have developed the concepts and text for this book with great passion and its brings us joy that readers find our work to be interesting and educational.

The concept of the sneak peak series was to create a series of guide books aimed at people in need of English in connection to technology. The goal was to create a "sneak peak" into the daily usage of such technology by native English speakers. The series boasted rich unaltered text by actual usage from a diverse community of English speakers. It began with emails and later moved on to forums and blogs. The next chapter of the sneak peak series brings users to the world of instant messaging. Recent smart phone applications helped create a faster method of instant communication through chat and internet calling applications such as Naver Line and Kakaotalk.

Unlike the previous two editions, where the user experienced looking into the English speakers' communication, this time we hope to give you access to phrases and terms that the an average Japanese user would like to know in English. Sneak Peak will come in handy to save you precious time while helping you enter the world of instant messaging in English, native style!

How the book is organized.

We collected text data among a variety of Japanese instant message users and analyzed the Japanese text to find the most appropriate English translation. The same Japanese phrase can become different phrases in English due to the difference in language and culture. We included our footnotes in our translations to provide further explanation to better understand those differences. The level of English is mostly casual due to the nature of instant messaging being among friends or friendly relations.

We sincerely wish you the best in your quest for English mastery and hope you enjoy this book as well as its benefits.

Nicholas Woo and the dedicated members of Ginko Labo

Table of Contents

7 Basic of Instant Messaging in English 8

Part I Conversation Samples 10

1. Greetings : Friends　あいさつ：友だち 11
2. Greetings : Friend overseas　あいさつ：海外の友だち 17
3. Greetings : Teacher and student　あいさつ：先生と生徒 23
4. Setting an appointment : Office friends　約束：社会人 29
5. Setting an appointment : Students　約束：学生 35
6. Setting an appointment : Party　約束：打ち上げ 41
7. Setting an appointment : Office dinner　約束：食事会 49
8. Changing an appointment : Friends　約束の変更：友だち 55
9. Changing an appointment : Work
　　　　　　　　　　　　約束の変更：バイトのシフト 61
10. Hanging out : Friends　遊ぶ：友だち 69
11. Asking a favor : Family　頼み事：家族 75
12. Asking a favor : Students　頼み事：クラスメート 81
13. Asking a favor : Friends　頼み事：友だち 87
14. Asking a question : Friends　質問：友だち 93
15. Making a decision : Students　決め事：学生 99
16. Daily chat : Study　日常会話：勉強 105
17. Daily chat : Food　日常会話：食事 111
18. Daily chat : Grandma　日常会話：おばあちゃん 117
19. Daily chat : Test results　日常会話：テスト結果 123
20. Daily chat : Theme park　日常会話：遊園地 129
21. Apologies : Late　謝る：遅刻 135
22. Apologies : Overslept　謝る：寝坊 141
23. Apologies : Cancel　謝る：キャンセル 147
24. Announcement : Concert ticket
　　　　　　　　　　　　お知らせ：コンサートチケット 155
25. Unknown sender : Strangers　送り主不明：知らない人 163

Part II　Useful phrases　168

1. あいさつ　169
2. 日にち・時間・時を表す表現　170
3. 驚き！の表現　172
4. お礼の表現　173
5. やさしい言葉をかける　175
6. 賛成・同意の表現　177
7. うれしい・楽しい表現　178
8. 否定・拒否の表現　179
9. 様子を伝える・説明する　182
10. 祝福・うらやましい　186
11. 天気・気温の表現　187
12. 怒り・不満の表現　189
13. 問いかけの表現　190
14. ほめる、ねぎらう表現　195
15. 程度表現　197
16. お願い・頼みごと　200
17. 命令形の表現　202
18. 返事・意思表示の表現　203
19. 気持ち表現　206
20. あやまる・お詫び　210
21. 悪態をつく・非難・あぶない・悪い表現　211
22. 人を表す表現　214
23. 性格・人柄を表す表現　215
24. 便利な言い回し表現　216
25. その他の便利ワード　219
26. 携帯電話　221
27. さようなら　222

7 Basics of Instant Messaging in English

1. 小文字：正しい英語は名前と文の最初の文字と I（私）を大文字にします。ですが、パソコンやスマートフォンでの場合いちいちシフトキーを押すのが大変なので、仲のいい友だちの場合は全部小文字で書くことがあります。ただ「めんどくさいから」だけではなく実際全部小文字にすることでメッセージを送るタイミングも早くなるので文法を気にした時より早いペースでおしゃべりができきます。

2. c, u：see と you になります。発音が同じなので、友達と話す時よくこの短縮形が使われます。ur, urs は your（または you're)、yours になります。また cu は「ク」ではなく see you と読みます。

3. lol：笑いを表現することが多いですが、元々の基本となっているのは LOL の短縮です。Laugh out loud（大きな声を出して笑う）の意味になります。使い方は日本語の（笑）と同じです。

4. 絵文字：英語のネイティブからみると日本の絵文字はすごいです。やり過ぎだと思う人もいるし、細かくて可愛いと思う人もいます。英語の場合、簡単な絵文字しかないので、日本語の絵文字はそのまま英語に表現できないことも多いです。英語でよく使う絵文字は :)「笑顔」;-)「ウィンク」:(「悲しい顔」:_(「泣いている顔」です。

5. 短縮語：LOL のように他にも短縮語がたくさんあります。普通の英語のネイティブでも分からない専門分野だけで使うものも多くありますが、一般的に掲示板などで使っている短縮語もたくさんあります。よく使うのは brb（Be right back すぐ戻る）imo（In my opinion 私の意見は、私の場合は）fyi（For your information お知らせです、言っとくけど）asap（As soon as possible なるべく早く、急いで）ttyl（Talk to you later また後でね、また話そう）などがあります。

6. 友達の間のチャットを見ると OK が k や Yes が yea になりますが、短縮語が使えるのは友達や冗談が言える仲の人のみです。目上の人に使いません。

7. 文の最初は大文字で書くことや「'」を使うことなどの細かい文法は無視することが多いです。ただし、これも友達に限ります。

Part I

Conversation Sample

1
Greetings:
Friends
あいさつ：友だち

鈴木先輩っ‼お久しぶりです！

鈴木先輩

久しぶりー！元気だった⁉

はいっ♪先輩部活は続けられてるんですか？

鈴木先輩

うん＼(^o^)／君は？

私も続けてます〜！あ、そういえば、ちか先輩はお元気ですか？同じ高校ですよね♪

鈴木先輩

うん、部活は続けてないけどね〜

> Suzuki!! Long time no see!

Long time no see は「お久しぶり」の決まり文句です。

> seriously! how have u been?

ここでの seriously は「まじめに」ではなく「あなたが言ったとおり」の意味で「お久しぶり」となります。
友だち同士で You が u になることがよくあります。

> Im doing good. are you still in the club?

Im は I'm です。パソコンやスマホでは「'」をよく省略します。

> yep. u?

Yep は Yes、Yeah と同じですが、簡単に短く答えている感じになります。

> me too! btw, how is Chika? ur from the same high school right?

btw は by the way の短縮語です。
ur は Your や you're です。

> yea. but shes not in the club anymore.

shes も Im と同じように「'」を省略しています。

そうなんですか！ちょっと残念です（´・ω・｀）

鈴木先輩

でも、バイト頑張ってるよ

なんだか、またみんなで集まりたいです！

鈴木先輩

そうだね、計画してみようかな…

お願いします‼

鈴木先輩

わかった‼じゃ、また連絡するね (^▽^)

はい！では、また！

> really? thats a bit of a shame

thats a shame、its a shame は「残念です」の決まり文句です。
a bit of 「ちょっと」

> but shes working really hard now.

> yeah, i really wanna meet up with everyone again

wanna は want to です。

> me too. ill try to get something going

ill も I'll の「'」を省略しています。
get something going は「何かを行くようにする」てはなく「何とかする」「何かを始める」です。

> please do!!

> leave it to me!! ill call u again later

普段「わかった」は Ok や I got it, alright などに訳されますが、ここでの「わかった」はニュアンス上「まかせて」と言っているので leave it to me（私にまかせておいて）とした方が自然です。

> ok! see you!

あいさつ★友だち

2
Greetings:
Friend overseas
あいさつ：海外の友達

 マイク

やあカオリ！

カオリ

やあマイク！長い間会ってないね。

 マイク

そうだね。久しぶり。カオリ最近どう？

カオリ

すごく楽しいよ＼(^o^)／お母さんたちは元気にしてる？

 マイク

うん！みんな元気。そういえば前に撮った写真送りたいんだけど住所教えて！

> hey kaori!

> yo mike! its been a while.

Its been a while または It has been a while、It's been too long は Long time no see と同じように「お久しぶり」の決まり文句です。

> yeah. long time no see. how r u these days?

How r u は How are you です。

> having lots of fun! is your family doing all right?

> yep. everyone is fine. btw, i wanna send those pictures we took last time. can i have ur mailing address?

btw は by the way の短縮語です。
wanna = want to

カオリ

写真楽しみにしてるよ〒000-0000 神奈川県相模原市南区相模大野0-000-0

 マイク

ありがとう。あとスケートした時の面白いムービーも送っとく（*^^*）

カオリ

ありがとう。すごく楽しかったね。また会いたいな

 マイク

僕もだよ。もうカオリは家族の一員だからいつでもおいで

カオリ

うん！マイクも来年絶対日本に来てね＼(^o^)／

 マイク

必ず行くよo(^▽^)o

> im looking forward to it. my address is post office number 000-0000, 0-000-0 Sagamiono, Minamiku, Sagamiharashi, Kanagawaken, Japan

im looking forward to ～または I look forward to ～は「前向きになる」ではなく「楽しみにしている」の決まり文句です。

> thanks. ill include that funny movie we took at the skate park.

> thanks. that was really fun! really miss u guys.

正しくは I really miss u guys です。このように「I」を省略することもあります。

> we do too. ur a part of our family now so come again anytime

ur は Your や you're です。

> ok! i hope you can visit japan next year too

> i will be sure to!

2 あいさつ★海外の友達

3
Greetings:
Teacher and student
あいさつ：先生と生徒

小島

佐々木先生、私です！小島ですo(^▽^)o

佐々木先生

おおー！！！小島か！

 小島

はいそうです！お久しぶりです

佐々木先生

久しぶりだな。最近はどうなんだ？

 小島

最近は楽しくやってます。

佐々木先生

そうかそれはよかった。テニスは続けてるのか？

 小島

もちろん！大会で優勝しましたよ！＼(^o^)／

Mr. Sasaki its me Kojima

Hey Kojima!

Hi. Long time no see.

Long time no see は「お久しぶり」の決まり文句です。

Yes it has been a while. How are you these days?

Its been a while も「お久しぶり」の決まり文句です。

I am having fun these days.

That is good to hear. Are you still playing tennis?

Of course! I won the tournament!

佐々木先生
> すごいな！！ずいぶん成長したんだな

 小島
> すごい頑張ってるので（*^^*）

佐々木先生
> そうかそうか。また今度、後輩たちに教えに来てくれよ

 小島
> はい！全然行きます！リカも一緒に連れて行きますね〜

佐々木先生
> それは助かる（^^）じゃあ待ってるな

 小島
> はいゞ（@^ー^@）ノ

> WOW! You must have gotten much better than before

> I really worked hard on it.

> I see. Maybe you can come visit your old school and help your juniors out?

old school は「古い学校」ではなく「母校」です。

> sure! I would love to! Ill bring rika along with me too

リカは人の名前なので r を大文字にして Rika と書くべきですが、ネットやチャットで仲がいい関係の場合、全部小文字にすることも多いです。

> that would be most helpful. then I will see you later

> good bye

ヾ(＠^ー^＠)ノ このように細かい絵文字は海外ではほとんどありません。日本の絵文字はとても細かくて可愛いと言われています。

4
Setting an appointment:
Office friends
約束：社会人の友だち

 IWAchi

つかれたー！Koko ー？

 IWAchi

いまどこ？あたし休憩中なんだけど

Koko

いま外回り終わって歩いてるとこ

 IWAchi

お疲れ様！今日の夜空いてる？

Koko

空いてるよ。どうしたの？

 IWAchi

久しぶりに飲み行こうよー

 IWAchi

愚痴聞いてよー（；；）

Koko

聞く聞く、8時くらいからでいい？

> **so tired! koko?**

(I am) so tired. チャットではよく短縮されます。

> **where r u? im taking a break for a few mins.**

r u : are you

> **i just finished the door sales and am on my way back**

> **oh cool. u free this evening?**

友だちの場合、Are you free this evening は短縮して u free? となることも多い。

> **yep. whatsup?**

yes の変わりに yep、Whats up がスペースなしで whatsup になります。「どうした？」の意味。

> **wanna go for a drink tonight?**

Do you want to go が wanna go になる。

> **i need to vent.**

vent は空気の動きの意味ではなく、不満を言う時の比喩として使われています。

> **k. im all ears. is 8 alright?**

im all ears は「私は全部耳です」ではなく「聞いてあげるよ」の意味。

 IWAchi

あたしは大丈夫！

 Koko

今日はおごるよ！どこ行きたい？

 IWAchi

え！いいよ！

 Koko

いいのいいの、じゃあお寿司にしよ！

 IWAchi

わかった！とりあえず仕事おわったら駅前待ち合わせね！

 Koko

了解！

> sounds good to me!

It sounds good → sounds good

> Its on me tonight. where u wanna go?

its on me : 奢る　　wanna = want to

> really? u dont have to do that!

u dont have to do that は「それをやる必要はない」ではなく「いいよ！」の意味。

> seriouslly, its fine. k, how bout sushi tonight?

how about - how bout

> Alright. Thanks. Anyways, lets meet at the station after work ltr.

ltr - later

> rgr!

roger (ok) → rgr

約束 ★ 社会人の友だち

5
Setting an appointment:
Students
約束：学生

Achu

まゆりん先輩、今お時間ありますか？

Mayurin

あるよ。どうした？

Achu

この前の論文のことなんですけど…明日時間大丈夫ですか？

Mayurin

そうだね。明日の午後ならいいよ。

Achu

ありがとうございます。

Mayurin

どこで会う？

Achu

どこでもいいですよ。

Hi Mayurin. Can you talk right now?

Sure. Whats up?

whats up? は「何が上にある？」ではなく友だちに使うカジュアルな挨拶です。
Hello や Good morning の代わりに使います。

Its about the paper we talked about last time... Do you have time tomorrow?

Oh yeah. Im alright in the afternoon.

Im = I'm

Thank you so much.

Where should we meet?

Anywhere is fine for me.

Mayurin

私もべつにどこでもいいけど。学校に来るの？

Achu

はい。行けます。

Mayurin

じゃ、学校前のコーヒーショップでいいんじゃない？

Achu

わかりました。何時にしますか？

Mayurin

発表が２時くらいに終わるから、２時半とかは？

Achu

はい。大丈夫です。

> I dont really care either. Will u be coming to school?

dont も Im と同じように「'」を省略しています。

> Yes. I can go.

> K then, why dont we meet at the coffee shop in front of the school?

K は OK の短縮です。

> Alright. What time should we meet?

> I finish my presentation at 2 so, how bout 2:30?

how bout は how about のネット上での短縮語です。

> OK. That sounds good.

6
Setting an appointment:
Party
約束：打ち上げ

あみ

体育祭お疲れ様♪（´▽`）

けん

お疲れ様！優勝惜しかったなー

あみ

本当悔しかった（T_T） でね、お疲れ様会みたいな感じで打ち上げやろうと思うんだ！

けん

おお！いいねいいね

あみ

だから男子に情報をけんが回してくれないかな？女子は私がやるから

けん

うん！わかった＼(^o^)／

> good job at the sports festival

> u2. it was a close one!

u2 は you too です。

> yea right? i thought we should have a closing party!

yea は yeah や yes。かなりカジュアルな表現なので友だちや親しい関係の人にしか使いません。

> ooh! that sounds good.

> so can u pass the news to the boys? ill call the girls.

正しい英語だと ill は I'll。文の流れを見て「病気」の ill なのか「I will」の ill なのかを判断しましょう。ここは I will の ill ですね。

> k, got it.

k は OK の短縮です。
ここの got it は I got it の省略です。意味は「もらった」ではなくて「わかった」になります。文の流れによって「受け取りました」や「気をつけます」などの意味もあります。

あみ

> ありがとう。でも何も決まってないんだよね（T_T）遊園地とかよりもご飯食べに行ったりする方がいいよね

けん

> そうだね。みんなその方が行きやすいと思うよ

あみ

> じゃあサイゼリヤでいいか！近いし＼(^o^)／

けん

> そうだねー！

あみ

> 日にちは振替休日の日かな？

> thanx. but we arent decided yet right? i think a meal would be better than going to a theme park.

thanx は thanks です。発音が同じになるので ks の代わりに x を使う人もいますが、若者のネット用語のイメージです。
arent = aren't

> yeah. that would make it easier to get everyone.

> k, how about saize? its close.

> yeah!

> meet on the makeup holiday?

正しくは Shall we meet~ から始まるべきですが、書かなくても意味が通じるので省略しています。

けん

うん！もちろん

あみ

時間は部活あるひともいるから夜ね
＼(^o^)／

けん

わかりましたーじゃあなんて男子に連絡すればいい？

あみ

6/27の6:00にサイゼリヤの前で待ち合わせで♪(´▽`)

けん

了解(*^^*)

> yes of course.

> some guys have clubs so we should meet in the evening

> ok. so ill tell all of the boys then right?

ill = I'll

> 6/27 6pm. meet up in front of saize

> rgr

rgr = roger

7
Setting an appointment:
Office dinner
約束：食事会

Extra 7:
この会話は社内の同僚との会話になるので、友だちとの会話よりスラングやネット用語は少なくなります。基本的に目上の人、ネット用語がわからない人、冗談が言えない内容の時などは省略、スラングなどは使わないほうがいいでしょう。

9月15日の夜7時から食事会を開こうと思っているんですけど大丈夫ですか？

先輩

うーん。次の日に会議があって資料を作らないといけないからちょっと無理かな。

他に空いてる日とかありますか？

先輩

17日の7時は？

その日は来れる人が少なくてやめたんです。

先輩

そっかー。そしたら20日なら平気よ。

本当ですか？その日ならみんな空いてるみたいですし、たぶん20日になると思います！

> We are planning on having an office dinner on Sep 15th 7pm. How is your schedule.

> hm... I have a meeting the next day and need to prepare some materials so I don't think I can make it.

> Is there another day you would prefer?

> How about 7pm on the 17th?

> That is not possible because too many people cannot come :(

:(は悲しい顔で、:) は笑顔です。

> I see. I am also free on the 20th.

> Really? I think most of our members should be open that day. I think the 20th should be fine.

ここでの open は「開ける」「営業を始める」ではなく free の代わりに使っています。つまり、この should be open は should be free「たぶん時間があるはず」や「空いていると思う」です。

先輩

わかった、20日空けておくね。

はい、お願いします。あと、どんなお店がいいか希望ありますか？

先輩

できるなら中華以外がいいかな。まあでも、みんなに合わせるわ。

わかりました、参考にします。

先輩

ありがとう。

詳しいことが決まったらまた連絡します。

先輩

待ってるね。

わかりました。

> OK. I will keep the 20th open.

ここでの open も free の意味です。

> Alright. Thank you. Also, do you have a preference on menu?

> I would prefer something other than Chinese if possible. But, I will follow the majority vote.

the majority vote は「多数の投票」と訳されますが、実際投票しているわけではなく「多数決」の意味になります。vote を省略して I will follow the majority だけでも意味は通じます。

> OK. I will keep that in mind.

keep that in mind (Keep 〜 in mind) は「参考にする」や「覚えておく」のような意味になります。Keep 〜 in my heart という表現もありますが、mind と違って heart は心の中に留める感じになるので、mind より感情や思考が強いイメージになります。この場面だと、ただのメニューの話なので mind ですね。

> Thanks.

> I will get back in touch once I have the details.

get back in touch は「戻って触る」ではありません！ get in touch, stay in touch は「連絡する」、「連絡を取り続ける」となり、back をいれると「また戻ってきたら連絡する」や「決まったらまた連絡する」になります。

> Alright.

> See you.

8
Changing an appointment:
Friends
約束の変更：友だち

> こんにちは！ゆり先輩、今平気ですか？

ゆり先輩
> こんにちは、大丈夫よ、どうしたの？

> お願いがあるんですけど、、

ゆり先輩
> うん？なになに？

> 今日の集合時間、4時から5時に変えられませんかねー？　仕事、終わらなくって（＞＜）？

ゆり先輩
> 全然いいよ！私もちょっと寄り道したかったの〜！

hello. Yuri? can you talk right now?

hi. yea sure. whats up?

yea は yeah や yes のかなりカジュアルな表現です。
whats up? は「何が上にあるの？」ではなく Hello の代わりの友だちに使うカジュアルな挨拶です。

I have a favor to ask.

ok. what is it?

can we change our meeting from 4 to 5? i think ill be working a bit overtime

ill = I'll

no problem. i have a couple of places to go too

本当ですか!? すみません🙇

ゆり先輩

いえいえ、気にしないで。場所はそのままお花屋さんの前で、大丈夫かな？

はい！ありがとうございます!!

ゆり先輩

はぁい！じゃ、あとで!!
お仕事頑張ってね♪

はい！先輩も！

> cool! sorry.

> dont worry about it. are we still meeting in front of the flower shop?

dont = don't

> yes! thank you.

> ok. so ill c u later. good luck with your work.

Ill → I'll
c u → see you
good luck は直訳すると「幸運」ですが、よく「頑張ってください」の意味で使います。

> ok. you too.

9
Changing an appointment:
Work schedule
約束の変更：バイトのシフト

Extra 9:

Chap 7より親しい関係のバイト先の友だちですが、一応仕事の話をしているのでスラングがいつもの会話よりだいぶ減っています。まりさんよりゆかさんの方がスラングを多く使っているのを見るとゆかさんの方が先輩か、またはフレンドリーな性格の人なのかもしれないですね。

まり
> ねーね、14日バイト入ってる？

ゆか
> 入ってないよー　でもなんで？

まり
> 私、用事があったのにバイト入れっちゃってさ、もしよかったら代わってくれない？

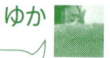

ゆか
> その日特に何もないからいいよ！何時から？

まり
> 4時から！ありがとう、ほんと助かった!!

> Hey! Are you working on the 14th?

>> Nope. Y?

Y は why です。

> I accidentally put in a shift for the 14th but I have something else to do that day. Would it be possible to switch shifts?

>> I dont have anything happening that day so its ok. wot time?

its = it's
wot は what ですが、イギリス的な発音になるのでアメリカではあまり使いません。

> 4pm! Thank you so much! You saved my life!

You saved my life を直訳すると「命の恩人です」、「命を救われました」ですが、ここで言いたいことは「本当に助かりました」です。

ゆか

いーえー　私この夏休み稼ぎたかったから（笑）

まり

給料はいったら何に使うの？欲しいものでもあるの？

ゆか

いやーお金貯めようと思っててね。

まり

えらっ！私絶対無理！服とかすぐ欲しくなって買っちゃうもん。

ゆか

私もだよー。でも我慢するって決めたの！

> No worries. I planned on saving as much as I can this summer anyway. lol

No worries は「大丈夫です」や「気にしないで」の意味。アメリカ人よりもオーストラリア人がよく使う表現です。

> What are you saving up for? Is there something u wanna buy?

wanna → want to

> Nah. I though of just saving.

Nah は No と同じ意味ですが「いいえ」より「いや（ないね）」のニュアンスがあります。

> Wow! I could never do that. I always end up buying clothes and stuff.

stuff は「何かを」と直訳されますが、文の流れによってその「何か」が変わります。ここだと clothes and stuff は「服とか」、「服など」に訳されます。

> Me too. but i decided to try my best to hold it in.

約束の変更 ★ バイトのシフト

65

まり

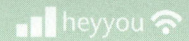

見習わなきゃ（笑）

ゆか

とにかく、いっぱいバイト入ってがんばるの！

まり

そっか、がんばって！じゃあ、14日お願いします。

ゆか

はーい（＊＾＾＊）

9 約束の変更★バイトのシフト

> i should learn from u lol

u → you

> anyway, i am filling my schedule with as much as work as I can!

> I see. good luck! Thanks for the 14th!

> Byebye

10
Hanging out:
Friends
遊ぶ：友だち

Extra 10:

この２人はずいぶんと省略形を使っています。でも、とても親しい友だち関係なのでお互い意味はちゃんと通じています。

さとし
> 今からどっか遊び行かない!?

だいすけ
> いいよ!!

さとし
> どこ行く？

だいすけ
> どこでも大丈夫だよ。ただ、超腹減ったから飯安くてうまいとこがいいなぁ！

さとし
> じゃあ町田行かね!?

だいすけ
> OK！

> **hey, wanna hang out today?**

wanna = want to
hang out は「遊ぶ」、「一緒にぶらぶらする」、「一緒に時間をつぶす」です。

> **sure!!**

> **where u wanna go?**

正しく書くと Where do you want to go（Where do u wanna go）ですが、do を抜いても意味は通じるので省略しています。

> **dont care really. but, im starving right now so i wanna go some place cheap but filling.**

dont care = I dont care
dont = don't

> **k, meet at Machida?**

k = OK
Shall we meet at Machida になりますが、Shall we を抜いても意味は通じるので省略しています。

> **ok!**

遊ぶ ★ 友だち

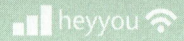

さとし
> とりあえずNICKオススメのカレーの店行こうぜ

だいすけ
> よっしゃあ！ いっぱい食ったら次は買い物だな

さとし
> そうだな。

だいすけ
> ゲーセンとかも行こうぜ

さとし
> もち

だいすけ
> 今日も大量GETだな（笑）

> anyway, lets go to that curry place nick was talking about

> all right! shopping after food right?

正しくは We are going shopping after food ですが、We are going を抜いても意味は通じるので省略しています。

> yea

> i also wanna stop by the arcades

arcade center はショッピング街などの賑やかな道や広場の意味ですが、ここでは arcades と省略したことでゲームセンターの意味になります。

> k

k → ok

> im gonna win some more stuff today. lol

im = I'm
gonna = going to
stuff の直訳は「何かを」ですが、文の流れによってその「何か」が変わります。ここでは「ゲームセンターの商品」です。

11

Asking a favor:
Family members

頼み事：家族

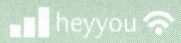

Yui
やほー 今何してんの？

Papa
べつにテレビ見てたんだけど…

Yui
パソコン壊れちゃったから直してよ。来れる？

Papa
今？

Yui
今だよ。いいじゃん。お願い。宿題できないの！＞・＜

Papa
今さ、サッカー面白いところだからやだよ。

Yui
サッカーなんて録画してあとで見ればいいじゃない。

> hey! u busy?

正しくは Are you busy または r u busy ですが、Are（r）を省略しています。

> Not really. Just watching TV.

Not really の直訳は「本当ではない」ですが、ここでは「べつに」。
正しくは I am just watching TV。

> my pc broke down. can u come over and fix it?

> now?

> yea, now. ur not busy right? please! i cant do any of my homework! :_(

yea は yeah や yes。かなりカジュアルな表現です。
ur は Your または you're です。ここでは you're です。
:_(は泣いてる顔です。日本の T.T のように使います。

> yea but the soccer game is getting exciting.

> cant u just record the game watch it ltr?

ltr = later

Papa

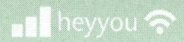

めんどくさいから明日にして。

Yui

じゃ、もし今来てくれるんだったら手料理ごちそうするよ。

Papa

本当に？じゃ、行こうかな？

Yui

マジで？やったね！ありがとう！

Papa

料理楽しみにしてるから。

Yui

はーい。じゃ、待ってまーす！

Papa

後でね。

> feeling lazy right now. cant we do it tmrw?

I am feeling lazy の I am を省略。
cant → can't　　tmrw → tomorrow

> ok, if u come over and fix this now, ill cook u dinner.

ここも「病気」の ill ではなく、I will の省略形ですね。

> really? alright then! shall we go?

Shall we go を直訳すると「一緒に行きますか？」となりますが、ここでは「行くよ」を少し面白く言うためにわざと使っています。

> really? awesome! Thank u!

> looking forward to your cooking.

I am looking forward to の I am を省略。

> sure! ok, ill be waiting!

> c u ltr.

c u ltr は see you later です。

11 頼み事★家族

12
Asking a favor:
Classmates
頼み事：クラスメート

みさき
ねぇ！ゆうだい！助けて！

ゆうだい
どうしたの!?　みさき？

みさき
宿題が終わらないよ〜

ゆうだい
なんだ、そんなことか…

みさき
本当に大変なんだって！わかんないよー

ゆうだい
はいはい、わかった。うちにおいで、教えてあげるから！

Yudai! HELP!

日本語の「ねぇ！」をそのまま訳すると hey、yo、oi などになりますが、名前を呼ぶ時は「ねぇ」の訳は省略した方が自然です。

whats wrong Misaki?

whats → what's

i cant finish my homework

cant → can't

ah, homework...

日本語の「そんなことか」をそのまま訳すると is that it、its that is it などになりますが、英語では相手の用件をくり返して言うのが自然です。

im serious! i dont know what im doing.

im と dont は I'm と don't になります。

k k, dont worry. if u want, u can come over. ill explain for u

k = ok
u = you
ここも「病気」の ill ではなく、「I will」の省略形ですね。

みさき
> ありがとう!!助かる〜

ゆうだい
> 今からこれる？

みさき
> うん、お菓子買ってくねー！

ゆうだい
> やった！待ってまーす！ちゃんと宿題も忘れずにね！

みさき
> わかってる〜！

ゆうだい
> じゃ、あとで!!

> **THANK YOU SOOO MUCH! you are a life saver**

気持ちを強く見せるために大文字を使うこともあります。良い意味でも悪い意味でも両方使います。また、大きい声で叫んでいるように強調して伝えたい時にも使います。ただ、使い過ぎるとテンションがすごく高い人に思われたり、オーバーアクションしているように見えるかもしれません。
life saver を直訳すると「命を助けた人」になりますが、ここでは感謝の気持ちを強く伝えるために使っています。

> **u comin now?**

are you coming、r u comin ですが、are (r) を省略しています。
u → you

> **yep. ill bring some snacks too.**

Yep は Yes、Yeah です。簡単に短く答えている感じがします。

> **nice! ill be home. dont forget to bring ur homework too.**

ur は Your または you're です。ここでは your です。

> **i know.**

> **k, c u**

c u は see you です。

13
Asking a favor:
Friends
頼み事：友だち

みさき: あーやば

ゆうだい: どうしたの？

みさき: 忘れちゃった！教科書

ゆうだい: 何に必要だったの？

みさき: 宿題でレポート書かなきゃいけなくて、必要だったんだよね

ゆうだい: えーそれはきついね。

みさき: うん、どうしよう（T_T）

> oh crap!

crapはそのまま使うと「コンチクショー」のように使います。物の代わりに使った場合「ゴミ」と訳した方が自然です。ただ、あまり良くない表現なので使うと言葉使いがきれいな人とは思われません。

> whats wrong?

whats → what's

> i forgot my textbook!

> what did u need it for?

> i need it for a report i have to write.

> hmm... thats tough.

thats = that's

> yea, what should i do?

ゆうだい

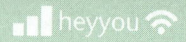

あ！もしかしたら俺今家にあるかも！探してみようか？

みさき

いいの？？

ゆうだい

うん。もちろん

みさき

本当？ありがとう。じゃあお願いします o(^▽^)o

ゆうだい

じゃあまた連絡するね

みさき

わかったー！

> hey! i might have mine at home! should i look for it?

> can u??

> yes. sure.

> really?? thank you. please.

> k, ill let u know ltr.

ltr → later → see you later

> alright!

14
Asking a question:
Friends
質問：友だち

りさ
> 久し振りー！

ゆうか
> 久し振りっ♪元気だった？

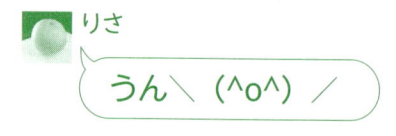

りさ
> うん＼(^o^)／

ゆうか
> あ、そういえば、聞こうと思ってたことが…

りさ
> なに、なに？

ゆうか
> DASNIって水、日本にあるか探したんだけど見つからなくて…そっちは普通に売ってるよね？

> long time no talk!

メッセージやチャットの場合、決まり文句の Long time no see（久しぶり）を long time no talk と言うこともあります。

> long time! how are you?

long time は long time no talk の返事として「久しぶり」になります。

> Im good.

Im → I'm
Im good は how are you の返事として「元気にやってるよ」の意味です。

> come to think of it, there was something i wanted to ask...

come to think of it は「そういえば」の決まり文句です。

> what is it?

> I was looking for a brand of water called DASNI in Japan but couldnt find it... its common over there right?

its → it's

りさ
そうなの〜？あるある、普通にあるよ？

ゆうか
やっぱり？美味しいから買いたくてさー

りさ
それなら送ってあげようか？

ゆうか
本当にっ!? いいの〜？

りさ
いいよ〜（^ー^）気にしないで！

ゆうか
ありがとう!!本当にありがとう

りさ
いいえ〜（*´∇｀*）じゃ、そのうちつくと思う（^ー^）

really? yeah. its common here.

i thought so. i really like it and was trying to find a way to buy some.

shall i send u some?

u → you

Really? could u?

its no problem. dont worry about it.

ここの dont worry about it は「心配するな」ではなく「気にしないで」です。

thank you sooo much! i really appreciate it!

thank you so much より強い感謝の気持ちを伝えるために so を強調して sooo と書いています。

dont mention it. ill send it to you soon. :)

ill → I'll
:) は笑い顔です。

15
Making a decision :
Students
決め事：学生

たくま

ふぅー。超疲れた。

ゆり

何？どうしたの？

たくま

今日さぁ、文化祭の企画を考えてたんだけどなかなか思いつかなくて…

ゆり

あ〜大変だね。お化け屋敷とか劇とかは？

たくま

いいね！自分的には食販とかもいいと思うんだよね！

ゆり

なるほどね！

> Ugh... I'm so tired.

ugh は疲れてくたくたを表現している効果音です。

> hey. whats wrong?

whats → what's。whats wrong は直訳すると「何が問題だ」ですが、ここでは「どうしたの」と訳すのが自然です。

> today, i was thinking about what to do for the school festival but couldnt come up with anything...

come up with~ は「~を思い出す」です。例えば come up with a good idea は「いいアイデアを思い出す」になります。

> i see~ tough times. how about just doing a haunted house or play?

tough times は festival preparation season is a tough time の省略。

> yea, that sounds good. but i was thinking that a food stand would be great!

yea は yeah や yes。かなりカジュアルな表現。

> I see

たくま
まとめるの難しいなぁ　どうしよ〜!?

ゆり
とりあえず候補をいくつか出してみて今度みんなで考えてみない!?

たくま
いいね！じゃあとりあえず今日は各自で考えてくるということで！

ゆり
了解。

たくま
またね

ゆり
うん。バイバイ

> its tough trying to put everything together. what should i do?

> anyway, how about just thinking of the options right now and deciding it with everyone later?

> good idea! k, then ill just think up some ideas on my own today then!

I will → I'll → ill

> ok

> c u ltr

c u ltr → see you later

> k, byebye

16
Daily chat:
Study
日常会話：勉強

こうき
やばいテスト1週間前なのになんもわからん

あきら
お前計画性がなさすぎんだよ（笑）

こうき
うっせ

あきら
何だと!? 心配していってやってんのに

こうき
ほっとけ

料金受取人払郵便

牛込局承認
8796

差出有効期間
平成31年3月
2日まで

（切手不要）

郵便はがき

162-8790

東京都新宿区
岩戸町12レベッカビル
ベレ出版

　　読者カード係　行

お名前		年齢
ご住所　〒		
電話番号	性別	ご職業
メールアドレス		

個人情報は小社の読者サービス向上のために活用させていただきます。

ご購読ありがとうございました。ご意見、ご感想をお聞かせください。

● **ご購入された書籍**

● **ご意見、ご感想**

● 図書目録の送付を　　　　　　　□ 希望する　　□ 希望しない

ご協力ありがとうございました。
小社の新刊などの情報が届くメールマガジンをご希望される方は、
小社ホームページ（https://www.beret.co.jp/）からご登録くださいませ。

> oh crap. 1 week before the test and i have no idea

crap はあまり良くない表現です。

> u need to learn to plan things better lol

u = you

> whatever

whatever は直訳すると「何でも」という意味になりますが、ここでは「うっとうしい」「うざい」のようなニュアンスになります。友だち同士では使います。

> what? im worried about u man

im → I'm
ここで man は「男」ではなく「〜ってんだよ」や「〜ってんのに」のようなニュアンスを入れるために使っています。ただ、目上の人に使うと失礼にあたるので使う範囲は友だちだけです。この会話の場合「にーちゃんよ」「兄弟」のように使っています。

> let it be

あきら

いんだな!? じゃあもういいや

こうき

うそです！ゴメン

あきら

反省しろ

こうき

はい！よかったら一緒に勉強させてください
(^^)

あきら

かまわんよ

こうき

よし！お願いします

あきら

OK！頑張ろう

> really? k, whatever u say man.

whatever you say は直訳すると「あなたが言った通り」ですが、この会話の流れでは「かってにしろ」「好きにしろ」「もういい」のような表現になります。

> no no im just kidding. sorry.

im → I'm

> think about it

> i will. if its not too much of a problem, do you mind if i study with you?

its → it's

> sure

> awesome! thank you so much.

> ok! good luck

17
Daily chat:
Food
日常会話：食事

さき
> 今日は食べ放題に行ったー！本当最高！

あみ
> えー！！いいな！どこの？

さき
> あのー…町田のおっきいビルの３階のお好み焼きやさん！

あみ
> うっそー！めっちゃ行きたかったところだ(T_T)

さき
> いいでしょー(*^^*)もう本当に美味しかった♥しかも、アイスも食べ放題ー！！

あみ
> まじで(T_T)まじでうらやましい…

さき
> じゃあ今度一緒に行こうよーo(^▽^)o

> i went to a buffet today. it was AWESOME!

AWESOMEが全部大文字なのは大きい声で叫んでいるように強調しているから。

> whoa! lucky! which buffet?

whoaは「すごい！」または「ええ？」です。

> um... its on the 3rd floor of that big building in machida. okonomiyaki place

its → it's

> no kidding! i really wanna go there

no kiddingは「うそ！」「本当に？」「まじで？」の意味でよく使います。
wanna → want to

> yeah right? its really good. on top of that, ice cream is all you can eat as well!!

アメリカでは食べ放題を 'all you can eat' とよく言います。

> seriously? im so jealous...

> well, lets go together someday then!

あみ

うん！行く行くー！！！

さき

じゃあ私は行ったばっかだから卒業祝いの時に行こうかー（*^^*）

あみ

うひょーo(^▽^)o楽しみ〜

さき

食べすぎて太るなよー笑

あみ

そのためにダイエットしとくから！（ ̄ー ̄）どや

さき

うっそーん！じゃあうちもしなきゃ(´⊙艸⊙｀;)

あみ

いえーい！食べ放題のためにダイエット頑張ろうー！笑

さき

頑張ろうー！＼(^o^)／

> yeah! lets go for sure!

k, since i just got back from it today, lets go together around graduation

> yay! lookin forward to it

正しくは I am looking forward to。

dont over eat and get fat now lol

dont → don't

> ill diet ahead of time just for that

I will → I'll → ill

u got to be kidding! maybe i should too.

u → you

yay! good luck to the both of us on our diet for buffet! lol

yay!

ここでの yay は相手の「頑張ろう」に同意しています。「おう！」という感じ。

18
Daily chat:
Grandma
日常会話：おばあちゃん

Extra 18:

前は祖父や祖母とチャットする機会が少なかったですが、最近スマートフォンでLINEなどを使うお年寄りも増えています。ただ、ネットのスラングはあんまり使っていません。この会話もおばあちゃんとの会話なのでスラングが少ないです。

おばあちゃん

お久しぶりです。元気ですか？

おばあちゃん！元気です（*^^*）

おばあちゃん

ちゃんと学校に行ってるのかい？

うん！行ってるよ。そういえばこの前送ってくれた荷物届いたよ！ママがありがとうだって

おばあちゃん

そうかい。団子はもう食べたかい？

食べたよ。とても美味しかった！一番あんこの味が美味しかったなあー

おばあちゃん

それはよかった。じゃあまた今度誕生日にでも送ろうかな。

> long time no see. how are you?

Long time no see は「お久しぶり」の決まり文句です。

> grandma! im well.

Im → I'm

> and how is school?

> school is good. by the way, we got your package the other day. mom said thanks.

> thats good to hear. did you try the dango?

thats → that's

> yes i did. it was really good! i think anko tasted the best.

> im glad to hear that. in that case, ill send some more on your birthday.

Im → I'm　I will → I'll → ill

やった！あのお店のは格別美味しいんだよね！ありがとう！！

おばあちゃん
いえいえ。じゃあ部活も頑張って、お母さんの手伝いもちゃんとするんだよ。

うんわかったー！部活はがんばってるからね！

おばあちゃん
また時間があったら遊びに来なさい。

今度の休みに行くかもです！

おばあちゃん
わかりました。それでは (*^^*)

> yeah! that store sells the best sweets! thank you!

> my pleasure. now then, good luck with your club activities. be sure to help out your mum too.

Mother の省略形はアメリカでは mom イギリスでは mum になります。

> i will! ill do my best at club too.

> if you have the time, feel free to come over.

feel free to ～は「いつでも～していい」です。例えば feel free to come over は「いつでも遊びに来てね」になります。

> ill stop by when i have a day off next time!

> ok. then, i will see you later.

19
Daily chat:
Test results
日常会話：テスト結果

かずや

やあ！

みずき

やあ (*^^*)

かずや

てかてか、今回のテストできた？

みずき

えー((((;゚Д゚))))))できないに決まってるー(T_T)

かずや

だよねーやっぱ？

みずき

まじ死んでるー。絶対赤点

> **yo**

yo はもともと hiphop 文化から流行した呼び方で hey と同じ意味ですが一般的には使われていません。Rap の曲の中でよく聴くことができます。

> **hey**

> **hey, did u do well on the test?**

u → you

> **Did i do well?? obviously not!**

日本語では「えー」だけで気持ちが通じますが、英語では全部言わないと通じないことも。Did i do well?? のように相手が言ったことを繰り返して表現します。

> **thought so...**

正しくは I thought so ですが、I がなくても意味は通じるので省略しています。

> **drove me crazy. im sure i failed.**

正しくは It drove me crazy です。

かずや
うちもだよー！6番の問題とか本当無理

みずき
あー！そこは自信あるんだよねー！どや！

かずや
うそー！みずきちゃん天才じゃん

みずき
でしょでしょ＼(^o^)／

かずや
勉強しなきゃなー

みずき
そうだね。受験もあるしがんばんなきゃ！よーし！！o(^▽^)o

かずや
お互い頑張ろうぜー

same here! i was clueless on #6.

oh! im sure i got that one!

u gotta be kidding me! ur a genius.

u は you、ur は you're です。

i am right? lol

i really should study.

i guess so. we have college entrance coming up so we should do our best.

yeah. best of luck for us both!

20
Daily chat:
Theme park
日常会話:遊園地

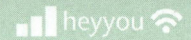

あや
> 今日遊園地行ったんだ〜

ちさ
> 本当にー？いいなー

あや
> すごい楽しかった！でも途中雨降っちゃって…(T_T)

ちさ
> そうだったの？たいへんだね

あや
> うーん。だから途中から水族館行ったんだよね〜。

ちさ
> えっ、さらに羨ましい！2個も楽しめるなんて！

> i went to the theme park today

> really? sounds like fun.

正しくは That sounds like fun ですが、That がなくても意味は通じるので省略しています。

> it really was! but it started raining in the afternoon...

> really? that doesnt sound fun.

doesnt → doesn't

> yea. so we went to the aquarium half way.

> actually, i envy that! u had 2 events in one day!

あや

> その時にイルカが可愛くてさo(^▽^)oだからエミに人形お土産で買って来たよ

ちさ

> ありがとうめっちゃ嬉しい！！もらったら飾ろうっと

あや

> いやいや、でかいから無理だよ〜

ちさ

> じゃあ、まくらにしよー＼(^o^)／

あや

> 喜んでくれてよかったよ、あとで渡すね

ちさ

> ありがとー

> the dolphin was really cute. so i got a little doll as a souvenir for u

u は you です。

> thank you! thats so nice! im gonna keep it on display. lol

thats → that's

> it might be a bit too big for that lol

> k, then use it as a pillow!

正しく書くと then I will use it as a pillow ですが、I will がなくても意味は通じるので省略しています。

> im glad u like it. ill pass it to you later.

> thanks

21
Appologies:
Late
謝る：遅刻

Extra 21
先輩と後輩の会話です。先輩に対して後輩は遅刻したことを謝っている状況なので、スラングはあまり出ていません。

Bucho!

待ち合わせの時間は 12:00 です。来れそうにない人は連絡ください。

unajuu~

私は時間に間に合います！

Bucho!

わかりました。みんなはもう来ていますが大丈夫ですか？

unajuu~

あっ！すみません。やっぱり時間に遅れそうです

Bucho!

なぜですか？

unajuu~

忘れ物を取りに家に帰って、やっと電車に乗れたと思ったら反対方向ので…
本当にすみません！

Bucho!

わかりました。もうそれは仕方のないことなのでまた後で聞きます。後どのぐらいで着きそうですか？

> we are meeting up at 12. please let me know if you cannot come.

>> ill be there on time!
>> I will → I'll → ill

> roger
> everyone is here. will you be on time?

>> sorry! i think im going to be late.
>> Im → I'm

> why?

>> i had to go back home to get something. i just got on the train but its the wrong direction... really sorry!
>> its → it's

> ok. there is nothing you can do about it now so we will talk later. around what time will you be here?

📶 heyyou 📶　　　　12:10

unajuu~
はい。えっと、30分はかかりそうです

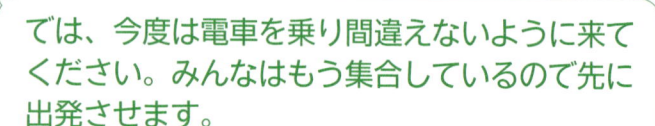

本 Bucho!
では、今度は電車を乗り間違えないように来てください。みんなはもう集合しているので先に出発させます。

unajuu~
わかりました。着いたらどうすればよいですか？

本 Bucho!
塔の下に私が待っているので、塔に来てください。場所はわかりますか？

unajuu~
ちょっとわからないかもしれないです

本 Bucho!
では、私が駅まで行くので改札にいてください。

unajuu~
わかりました！

ok. um... I think its gonna take 30 minutes to get there.

gonna → going to

please be careful to get on the right train next time. since everyone else is here, we will go ahead.

ok. what should i do after i arrive?

ill be waiting at the pagoda. please come there. do you know where it is?

i might not

then, ill meet you at the station turn stile.

ok!

22

Appologies:
Overslept

謝る：寝坊

ゆうか
集合時間 6:00 だけどまだ？

まゆ
ごめん！今起きた！（(((;゜Д゜))))))

ゆうか
寝坊したのー？

まゆ
うんそう！やばい

ゆうか
えーみんなもういるよ？

まゆ
うそ！どうしよう（T_T）

ゆうか
何時くらいに早くて来れる？

まゆ
急いで準備してもそっちに着くの 8:00 くらいになっちゃうかも

22 謝る★寝坊

> ur supposed to be here by 6. when will u get here?

ur → you're

> SO SORRY! I JUST woke up!

JUST を大文字にしたのは今起きたばっかりだと強調するためです。

> overslept?

> yea. OMG

OMG は Oh My God, Oh My Gosh の省略です。

> everyone else is here u know

> really? what should i do?

> if u hurry, when can u be here by?

> even if i hurry, i think itll be around 8.

itll → it will

ゆうか
ああ。そうなのかー…

まゆ
遅くなっちゃうから先に向かってていいよ。ごめんね

ゆうか
いや、大丈夫だよ。待ってるから

まゆ
え申し訳ないな。

ゆうか
買い物とかでみんなで時間潰してるから全然大丈夫

まゆ
ありがとう。急いで行くね

ゆうか
うんわかった＼(^o^)／

> ah... i see...

> im gonna be late so u guys can go ahead without me. really sorry.

really sorry は I am を省略。

> nah, its ok. we'll wait up.

nah は no と同じ意味ですが、かなりカジュアルな表現なので友だちや親しい関係の人にしか使いません。ニュアンスは「いいよ」「大丈夫だよ」に近いです。
its → it's

> i cant do that to you.

cant → can't

> we can just kill some time shopping so its ok.

kill time は「時間をつぶす」。

> thank you. ill hurry.

I will → I'll → ill

> ok.

23
Appologies:
Cancel
謝る：キャンセル

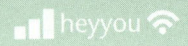

はな
あのさ、30日会う約束してたじゃん？

あい
そーだね！それがどうかしたの？

はな
ごめん、あいに会えなくなっちゃった

あい
何かあったの？

はな
実はね、バイトの子が風邪引いちゃって店長にどうしても出てくれって言われちゃって。

あい
そーなんだ。別にいいよ（*＾＾*）

23 謝る★キャンセル

> hey.. about our meeting on the 30th...

> yeah? something wrong?

正しくは Is something wrong。Is を省略。

> Sorry. I cant go.

cant → can't

> something happen?

正しくは Did something happen。Did を省略。

> the thing is, someone from my work place got sick and the manager insisted that I fill in.

the thing is は「それは」より「実は」に近いです。
「どうしても〜と言う」は insist that または insist on です。

> i see. its alright.

its → it's

はな

ほんとごめんね。あいと久しぶりにいろんなこと話せると思ったのに（TT）

あい

しょうがないいよ！じゃあ、近いうちに空いてる日ない？

はな

ありがとう。えーっとね、2日空いてるよ。

あい

2日は私がだめだな、他の日はどう？

はな

じゃあ4日は？

あい

午後からでもいいなら平気！

23 謝る★キャンセル

> really sorry! I really wanted to meet and catch up cause its been a while :(

catch up は「捕まる」ではなく「いろんなことを話す」です。個人的な話の時だけに使います。 :(は悲しい顔です。

> but it cant be helped right? anyway, any other day ur free?

ur → you're

> thanks. let me see... how bout the 2nd?

let me see は「見せて」にもなりますが、ここでは時間稼ぎの表現で使っています。

> sorry, the 2nd wont work for me. any other day?

wont → won't

> k. how bout the 4th?

how bout は how about です。かなりカジュアルな表現になります。

> the afternoon is ok!

はな

ほんとに？ そしたら4日の1時に駅のカフェでいい？

あい

いーよ！

はな

やった！あいに早く会っていろいろ話したいよー

あい

私も！4日楽しみにしてるね。

はな

うん！ 30日はほんとごめんね？ じゃあまたね。

あい

ばいばーい！

> cool! then, the 4th 1pm at the station cafe?

> sounds good!

sounds good は「いい音」ではなく「いいね」や「いいよ」になります。

> cool! i really want to catch up on things

> me too. looking forward to it.

I am looking forward to it の I am が省略されています。
Looking forward to ~ は「前を見る」ではなく「楽しみにしている」です。

> yep. really sorry bout the 30th. see u soon

正しくは I am really sorry。
sorry bout は sorry about です。とてもカジュアルな表現です。

> bye bye

24
Announcement:
Concert ticket
お知らせ：コンサートチケット

クミ
>【拡散希望】西野カナのコンサートのチケットが余っているので行ける人返信ください！

えみ
>もし予定が合えば行けるのでもしよければ譲ってください！

クミ
>まじですか！えっと、8/24の18:00です！2枚余ってます。

えみ
>行けますー＼(^o^)／友だちと一緒に行きたいので2枚よければ！

クミ
>わかりました！本当ありがとうございます＼(^o^)／料金なんですが…

お知らせ☆コンサートチケット

Hey everyone! I have some left over tickets for Nishino Kana's concert! Let me know if anyone is interested!

I wanna go if my schedule fits. When is it?

wanna → want to

Really? Let me see... its on August 24th, 6pm. I have 2 tickets left.

its → it's

Great! I wanna bring my friend along too. Can I have both tickets?

OK! Thank you so much. now, about the cost...

えみ

いえいえこちらこそ (*^^*) はい (汗 高すぎるとちょっとあれなんですけど (T_T)

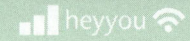

クミ

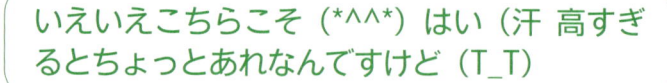

半分のお金で大丈夫です！

えみ

えっ！いいんですか！？？

クミ

ええ＼(^o^)／全然大丈夫です！貰い手がいるだけでありがたいので (*^^*)

えみ

なんかすみません (T_T)

SORRY…

> I should be thanking you. Yeah?（I hope it isnt too expensive）

isnt → isn't

> Half price is good for me.

> Huh? Really? It that really enough?

huh?「えっ？」はカジュアルな表現なので友だち同士だけで使います。

> Its perfectly fine. im just glad to have found someone going. :)

its → it's　im → I'm　:) は笑い顔です。

> Thank you so much.

クミ
じゃあ、8/20 の 14:00 とか空いてますか？

えみ
大丈夫です

クミ
渋谷に来れますか？

えみ
すいません。渋谷ではなく新宿でも大丈夫ですか？

クミ
大丈夫ですよ (*^^*) では 8/20 の 14:00 に新宿の駅で！

えみ
わかりました。

24 お知らせ★コンサートチケット

> k, u free at 2pm on 8/20?

正しく書くと are you free（r u free）ですが、are（r）を抜いても意味は通じるので省略しています。

> yes.

> can u come to Shibuya that day?

> sorry but could we meet at Shinjuku instead?

> sure. ;) so 8/20 2pm at shinjuku.

;) はウィンクしている顔です。

> got it!

got it は「もらいました」だけではなく「わかりました」にもなります。話の流れをみながら意味を判断してください。

25
Unknown sender :
Strangers
送り主不明：知らない人

こうへい

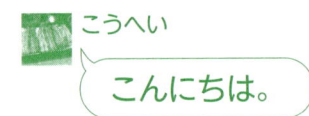

こんにちは。

しょう

こんにちは。どなたですか？

こうへい

先日お会いしましたよね

しょう

え？すみません。記憶が…

こうへい

食べ放題で戦った相手ですよ！！

しょう

ああー！思い出しました！まさかTwitterでお会いするとは！w

こうへい

ははは　あの時は楽しかったですね

しょう

ですね　また戦いましょうよ

25 送り主不明 ★ 知らない人

hello

hello. who is this?

we met the other day right?

really? sorry, i cant remember...

we fought at the all you can eat contest!!

ah! i remember now. i never thought id meet you on twitter! lol

I would を I'd に短縮してまた「'」を省略すると id になります。

hahaha, that was real fun.

yea it was. lets do it again someday.

こうへい

ぜひぜひ！望むところです

しょう

負けませんよ！笑　次はラーメンとかどうです？

こうへい

いいですね。私の大好物です＼(^o^)／

しょう

じゃあそういうことで。また詳しいことは後日決めましょう

こうへい

そうですね。たのしみにしてます

> **for sure! i look forward to it.**

「ぜひ」を直訳すると please ですが、この場合は「ぜひ」を「ぜったいそうしましょう」のように考えて英文を作ります。For sure は「確実に」とも訳せますがここでは「ぜひぜひ（行きましょう）」になります。
Im looking forward to ～または I look forward to ～は「前向きになる」ではなく「楽しみにしている」の決まり文句です。

> **i will not lose! lol should we go for ramen next time?**

> **sounds nice. ramen is one of my favorites.**

正しくは that sounds nice。that がなくても意味は通じるので省略しています。

> **k. then lets decide the details later some other day.**

> **ok. looking forward to it.**

Part II
Useful Phrases

Useful Phrases

1 あいさつ Greetings

おはよう
good morning / morning / hello

起きた？
r u up? / r u awake? / are you up? / are you awake? / sleeping? / still sleeping?

こんにちは
good afternoon / hello / hi

こんばんは
good evening / hello / hi

元気？
how are you? / are you alright? / how is it going? / how zit? / whats up? / was sup? / sup? / how r u? / u ok? / how have you been?

元気です
im fine / im doing good / its all good / not bad / doing alright

おい！
Oi!（アメリカではあんまり使ってません）/ Hey! / Yo!

169

最近どう？
How r u these days? / Hows it goin these days? / hows life? / how have you been?

最近何かありましたか？
Whats up these days? / anything new? / any news? / whatcha been up to? / Whats going on these days?

お久しぶりです
Long time no see / its been a while / long time no talk / been a while

2 日にち・時間・時を表す表現
Time related phrases

明後日
The day after tomorrow / 2 days from now

おととい
the day before yesterday / 2 days ago

上旬
beginning of the month / early January (February…)

中旬
middle of the month / mid January (February…)

Useful Phrases

下旬
the end of the month / the end of January (February…)

月末
the end of the month（英語では下旬と同じ）/ the last few days of the month / the very end of January (February…)

再来月
the month after next / two months later / in two months

真夜中
middle of the night / late night / deep into the night

夜明け
dawn / daybreak / sunrise

夕暮れ時
twilight / dusk / sunset

〜時頃
around ~ / about ~

いつでも
anytime / whenever / whenever you want / whenever is best

日常
every day life / daily life / everyday stuff / ordinary day / same old routine / daily routine

3 驚き！の表現　Exclamation phrases

あっ！
Oh no! / Crap!（目上の人には使いません）/ Shoot! / Ah!

あら！
Huh? / What? / Wait! / Wha? / Eh?

あらま
Oh dear / Oh no / Oops / Whoops / Aw shucks / Aww…

えっ？
Huh?

えー！？／すごい！
Whoa!

おっとっと
oops / whoa / yikes（びっくりした）/ that was close（あぶなかった）

Useful Phrases

しまった！
darn it! / crap! / shoot! / Oh no! / Doh!

うそ！／まじで？／本当？
no kidding!

信じられない！
i cant believe it! / you gotta be kidding me! / what?! / are you serious? / no way!

そんな！
you gotta be kidding! / no way! / not fair! / what?!

4 お礼の表現　Giving thanks

ありがとう／どうも
Thank you/ thanks / thank u / thanx / thnx / I appreciate it / Thank you so much.

こちらこそありがとう
No, thank YOU. (**YOU** をすべて大文字にしないと「結構です」という断る意味になってしまいます)

いろいろありがとう
Thanks for everything.

とにかくありがとう
Anyway, thank you.

ありがとうございました
Thank you for ~ / Thanks for ~ / thank u for ~ / thnx for ~ / I appreciate ~ the other day（yesterday など）

感謝します
I appreciate it / thank you / thanks / i am grateful

やさしすぎ！
You're so nice! / Thats so kind of you!

ありがたい
That'll be great. / ~ is a life saver.

なんて言ったらいいか
I don't know how to say it but … / I don't know how to put it but …

恩にきるよ
I am in your debt.

迷惑かけたね
Thanks for going through the trouble.

Useful Phrases

ごちそうさまでした
thanks for the meal / that was a good meal / that was good / im full / that was filling

助かるよ
you saved my life / you're a life saver / that saved my life / thank you / i really appreciate it / that would be (was) very helpful

5 やさしい言葉をかける
Encouragement and suggestions

落ち着いて
calm down（ゆっくりして欲しい時） / relax（緊張する時） / settle down（うるさい時） / quiet please（うるさい時）

気にしないで
dont worry about it / no worries / its fine / its ok / you're welcome / you dont have to / its all good

気をつけて
be careful / watch out / take care / take care of yourself / good luck

そんなことないよ
stop flattering me / you're too kind / aw, shucks

大丈夫
its ok / its alright / its fine / no problem / all is well / good as always / good as new

楽しみです
i look forward to it / im looking forward to it / sounds great / i cant wait / sounds wonderful

楽しんできてください
youre gonna love this / its gonna be great / ur gonna love it / its going to be great

楽しんでね
have fun / enjoy yourself

無理しないで
dont push yourself too hard / do it in good pace / pace yourself well / dont overwork yourself

お祈りします
Good luck（応援）/ Ill pray for you（宗教的）/ I wish you luck（応援）/ Best of luck to you（応援）/ I wish you the best（応援）/ You can do it（応援）/ I hope everything is ok（心配）/ I hope everything is fine（心配）

しっかりして
get a grip on yourself / wake up / get a hold of

Useful Phrases

yourself / get yourself together / stay awake / stay alert

（話を）聞くよ、聞いてあげるよ
I'm all ears. / im all ears.

6　賛成・同意の表現　Agreement and approval

うん
yeah / yea / yep / ok

いいですね！
Sounds nice! / That's a great idea! / Cool! / Nice! / Alright! / Right on! / That sounds good!

いいですよ
Any~ is fine for me
例：**Anywhere is fine**（どこでもいいですよ）

いいよ本当に/いいんだってば/いいのいいの
It's fine, really! / It's alright, don't worry about it / For real, its alright / Seriously, its fine

---

いいね！
That sounds good / Good idea / Great! / Yeah! / Right on! / Yes!

177

いいよ
Alright / No problem / Its ok (alright) / sure

賛成/同意します
i agree / i concur / im with you / vote me in / you have my vote / count me in

のった！
im in! / count me in!

7 うれしい・楽しい表現　Positive phrases

やった！／わーい！
yay! / yeah! / oh yeah! / hooray!

わお！
Wow! / Ohhh!

うれしい！
Thank you so much!（ありがとう）/ I'm so happy.

良かった！
Thank goodness.（あぶなかった）/ That's great.

最高！
Awesome! / Oh yeah!

Useful Phrases

しあわせ！
I'm so happy!

やったね！
Great! / Nice!

ラッキー！
Lucky! / That was fortunate.

ついてるー！
I'm rolling well. / I'm feeling lucky.

（笑）
lol / LOL / rofl / lmao / hahaha / hehehe

ｗｗｗ
lol / LOL / rofl / lmao / hahaha / hehehe

8　否定・拒否の表現　Negative phrases

あんまり
Not really / Not much / Nah / Nope / Not ~

しらん
i dunno / dunno (dont know)

やだ
no / nope / nah / i dont want to

やめて
Stop it. / Cut it out.

ありえない
No way! / That's BS / Impossible

違うよ
No / Nope / Not quite

まちがってるよ
That's wrong

悪いけど
Sorry but ~ / I don't mean to be rude but ~

無理です
thats impossible / thats too much / thats difficult / that wont work / that wouldnt work / we cant do that / its impossible

だめだ
its no use / its useless / its hopeless / i cant do it / i failed / its not working

Useful Phrases

いいよ（断る）
You don't have to do that!

〜してはいけない（だめだ）
you shouldn't 〜 / you cant 〜 / you're not allowed to 〜 / i wouldn't do that if i were you

賛成できない
I can't agree with that.

同意できない
I disagree / I can't agree.

勉強したくない
I don't wanna study / I'm tired of studying.

働きたくない
I don't feel like working. / I wanna relax. / I wanna take it easy.

私じゃない
Not me.

〜したくない
I don't wanna 〜. / I don't feel like 〜.

できれば〜したくない
I'd rather not ~ / I'd prefer not to ~.

そんなはずはない
No way. / impossible / That can't be right.

9 様子を伝える・説明する　Describing things

熱いです（話題が、人が）
This is hot / This is passionate / It's emotional / He (she) is on fire / He(she) is so passionate

疲れた
tired / i need a break / i feel knackered / i need some rest

やばい
OMG / crap / oh no

きつい
tough

しんどい
so tired / i need a break / im exhausted / im so knackered / i need some time off / i need rest

Useful Phrases

明らかにダメ
obviously not

慣れました
i got used to it / im used to it now

忙しい
Im so busy! / Busy.

眠い
sleepy / drowsy

のんびり
relax / laze around / take it easy / take it slow / chill / chill out

ゆっくり
slowly / steadily / take my time

簡単な
a simple ~ / an easy ~

難しい
difficult / hard / tough / challenging

時間がない
im busy / i have no time / there is no time / time is running out / we our running out of time

暇
bored / plenty of time / free

暇がない
busy / no time for anything / packed with stuff to do / no time to rest

どうでもいい
whatever / yeah, whatever

おなかすいた
im hungry / so hungry / im starving

油断した
i was careless / it was careless of me / it slipped by me

酔っ払い
a drunk / drunk person

酔っぱらった
im (he is, she is, they are, we are) drunk / i had too much to drink / i drank too much / i was plastered

Useful Phrases

気づいていない
not aware of ~ / oblivious to ~ / he (she, it) doesn't know / I (we, they) dont know

気づいている
aware of ~ / I (we, they) know / he (she, it) knows

センスいい
has (have) a nice touch / good taste / stylish / fashionable / classy

センス悪い
bad taste / horrible taste / no sense of style / no class

ウケる
thats funny / thats cool / thats nice / awesome! / right on!

ウケない
doesn't work / not getting it / lame / boring

盛り上がる
bring the atmosphere up / build the atmosphere / kick it up a notch / get the crowd involved / get everyone involved / get the people excited / get everyone pumped

盛り下がる／シラケる
kill the atmosphere / burn down the atmosphere / bore everyone / lose everyone's attention

10 祝福・うらやましい　Blessings and envy

おめでとう！
congratulations! / congrats! / gratz! / good job! / Good game.

おめでたい
great / worthy of celebration / noteworthy

やったね
Great! / Awsome! / Yeah!

さすがだね
（形容詞）as always / As expected.

うひょー
yay!

自分のことみたいにうれしいよ
I'm happy for you. / I'm glad you're happy.

Useful Phrases

お幸せに
I hope you're happy. / Best wishes.

喜んでくれてうれしい
I'm glad you like it.

いいなあ
I envy you! / Lucky! / That sounds like fun! / I wish I was there

うらやましいよ
I envy you. / I'm so envious.

まじでうらやましい…
I'm so jealous...

11 天気・気温の話題
Weather related phrases

いい天気だね
The weather is nice today / Fine weather today

雨ばっかりだね
Its raining a lot / Its raining cats and dogs / nothing but rain / rain all day

雲ってるね
its cloudy / the sky is cloudy / I see a lot of clouds today

台風が来るね
A typhoon is coming / Get ready for the typhoon

雪が降るかも
it might snow / it could snow / it could be snowy / we might have snow

さっきヒョウ（雹）が降ったよ
it was hailing earlier / we had hail this morning (a few minutes ago, an hour ago…)

暑い
It's hot / The weather is hot

すごい暑さだね
The heat is intense / its really hot / its too hot

寒い
its cold / im cold

こごえそう
its freezing / its really cold / its too cold / im freezing

Useful Phrases

涼しくなったね
it got cooler / its getting cooler / the weather is cooling off

暖かくなってきたね
it got warmer / its getting warmer / the weather is warming up

12 怒り・不満の表現
Irritation, dissatisfaction and discomfort

あっち行け
Go away / Get out of here（出てけ）/ Get lost!（ひどい表現）/ Scram!（相手を無視する表現）

おそい！
too slow!（動きが）/ too late!（間に合わない）/ faster! / quicker / hurry! / hurry up!

ばかな！
what the!? / What in the!? / Are you kidding me? / r u serious?

ばかばかしい
stupid / lame / dumb

恥ずかしい
embarrassing / shameful

腹が立つ
angry / pissed off

ふざけるな
screw that / no way / no way in hell / kiss my ass / kiss my butt / shut up / what the hell? / WTF

ほっとけ
let it be / leave it alone / leave me alone / give him (her, me, us) some space / give it some time

13 問いかけの表現
Confirming and asking questions

あなたはどう？
How about you? / how bout u? / how about ~?

いい？
Can you? / Can u? (13) Really? Is that ok? / For real?

いいの？
Really? / For real? / Seriously? / May I? / Can I? / Are you sure?

Useful Phrases

一緒に〜どう？
Shall we（動詞）together? / How about we（動詞）together?

一緒に行こう
lets go together / why dont we go together? / would you like to join me(us)? / why dont you join me(us)?

行こうよ/（私も）行くよ
Lets go! / I want to go / I wanna go / Im in! / Count me in!

来れる？
u comin? / r u comin? / are you coming?

すぐに来れる？
Can u come soon? / Can u come quickly?

いつ空いてる？
when are you free? / when r u free? / when can I meet you? / when can i meet u?

いつがいい？
what would be good for you? / when would you like to meet? / when is best for you?

何時？
what time is it? / whats the time?

今？
now? / right now?

手伝おうか？
do you need a hand? / can i give you a hand? / may i help you? / can i help u? / r u alright?

名前は？
whats your name? / whats ur name?

君は？
and you? / how about you? / how do you feel? / whats your opinion?

ここでいい？
is this aright here? / is this good here? / here?

これでいい？
is this enough? / is this good enough? / is this right?

これはどう？
how is this? / how about this? / what do you think about this?

Useful Phrases

だれ？
who are you? / who is that? / who r u? / who's that?

どうした？
whats wrong? / is everything alright? / r u all right? / whats the matter?

どう？
how is it? / is it ok?

どこから来たの？
where did you come from? / where did u come from?

どこから来るの？
where will you be coming from? / where r u coming from? / where r u at?

どこ住んでるの？
where do you live? / where do u live? / which station do you live near?（駅）/ which city are you from?（市）

どこの出身？
where are you from? / where were you born? / where did you come from? / where do you live? / where are you originally from?

どこ？
where is it? / where are you? / where r u? / where?

なぜ？
why is that? / why?

何？
what? / huh? / wot?

何て言ったの？
what did you say? / did you say something? / did you say anything?

どうかした？／何かあったの？
Something wrong?

ねえ？（でしょう？）
right?

本気？
are you serious? / r u serious? / for real? / do you mean it?

まじで？／本当？
seriously? / for real? / really? / are you kidding me?

Useful Phrases

わかった？
got it? / understand? / alright?

わかる？
do you understand? / do you know?

14 ほめる、ねぎらう　Praise

上手い
good / nice / smooth / skilled

おいしい/うまい
good / tasty / delicious / yummy / I like it

すごいね
thats amazing / incredible / wow

天才だね
you're a genius

きれい
pretty / beautiful / clean / nice / charming

かわいいね
cute / so cute / How cute!

かっこいいね
cool / so cool

クールだね
cool

おだいじに
Please be careful / take care / take care of yourself / stay safe / get well soon（病気の場合）/ i hope you get better（病気の場合）

大変だね
thats rough / that sounds tough / I'm sorry

ごちそうするよ
~ is on me / ill pay for ~ / ill take the tab / ill take the check

お疲れさま
good job / good work / nicely done / congratulations / great / nice / good

大丈夫？
Are you alright? / u ok?

無事？
u ok? / are you ok?

15 程度表現 Expressions related to the degree of something

まあまあ
now now / take it easy / relax / chill out / chill

ひどい（人が）
mean / cruel / horrible

ひどい（状況が）
terrible / bad / messy

すごく
really / extremely / very

かなり
quite / a good bit

とても
a lot / really

必ず
must

絶対に
definitely / absolutely

きっと
I'm sure ~

たぶん
I think ~ / Maybe ~

いつも
Always

たびたび
sometimes / from time to time

よく／頻繁に
quite often / often / frequently / a lot

たまに
sometimes / once in a while / every now and then

時々
from time to time / once in a while / every now and then

まれに
rare / uncommon

すぐに
now / immediately

Useful Phrases

間もなく
soon / immediately

そのうち
eventually / someday / oneday

ものすごく小さい
incredibly small / really small / ridiculously small / tiny

ものすごく大きい
incredibly big / really big / ridiculously big / giant / massive / humongous / huge

いっぱい
fill ~ up as much as I can / full / to its fullest / as much as I can / as ~ as I can / completely / all the way

たくさん
a lot / a bunch

ほどほど
don't over do it

少し
a bit / a little

ほんの少し
just a little bit

ちょっと
a bit / a little bit / a little / a tad / slightly

ちょっとだけ
just a little bit / just a tad / just a bit / just a bite / just a taste / just a small bit / just for a second

一発で
in one shot / in one go / in a single shot / in a single blow / in one try

16 お願い・頼みごと　Asking for help

手伝ってください
please help / can you give me a hand? / can u gimme a hand? / please lend a hand / help me please

ちょっと手伝って
Can u help me out? / Can u lend a hand?

頼んでもいい？
may i ask you a favour? / can i ask you for some help? / i have a favour to ask

Useful Phrases

教えて
please tell us / please let us know / please teach us / I want to know / I want to know when (where, how, why, who)

頼む！／お願い！
Help! / Please!

何とかして！
Do something!

一生のお願い！
please help me / save me

よろしくお願いします
thank you / good luck / i look forward to ~ / looking forward to ~

助けて！
help! / save me! / help me! / SOS! / gimme a hand!

ちょっと待って
hold on / wait up / wait a second / hold on a sec / please wait a moment

〜していい？
can you ~ ?

〜して欲しい
I'd like you to 〜

〜してくれる？
could you 〜 ?

17　命令形の表現　giving orders

急いで！
hurry! / hurry up! / come on! / quickly! / rush!

今だ！
now! / right now!

行け〜！
Go!

やってみて
Try it / Give it a go

心配しないで
Don't worry. / No sweat.

心配させないで
Don't scare me. / Stop messing around.

Useful Phrases

がっかりさせないで
Don't dissapoint me. / I'm expecting ~.（いい結果を期待している感じ）

勘弁してよ
Gimme a break. / Cut me some slack.

うぬぼれないで
don't be too conceited / stop bragging

我慢して
be patient / bear with it / you can do it

18 返事・意思表示の表現
Replies and explanation

いいえ（いや／大丈夫／どういたしまして）
Don't mention it / No problem / No worries / It's fine / It's ok / Nah

いいえ、結構です（断る）
No it's fine, thank you / No thank you

いいえ、別に
It's alright / It's fine / Don't worry about it / It's nothing

203

どういたしまして
dont mention it / its fine / youre welcome / no worries / my pleasure

かまいません
either way / either one is fine / it doesn't matter / its fine / sure / i dont care / whatever you want

そうだね
I guess so.

私も！
Same here!

まかせて！
leave it to me! / I can do it! / I can handle that!

もちろん
of course / definitely

それはよかったね
That's good to hear.

大丈夫です（断る）
thank you, but i must decline / sorry / its ok / its fine / no thank you

Useful Phrases

わかった
i got it / ok / got it / right / alright / all right / understood / roger / rgr

わかりません
i dont get it / i didnt get it / i dont understand

納得できない
i cant accept this / this is unacceptable / i refuse to believe this / this cant be right / this cant be true

納得できる
i can see that / i see / i can understand that / i understand / its understandable

すぐ戻るよ
ill be back soon / ill be back in a second / ill be back in a minute / gimme a sec / brb / be right back

全く知らない
I have no idea / im clueless / i dont know / im completely lost

19 気持ち表現 Feelings

楽しみ〜
lookin forward to it / I'm looking forward to it.

懐かしい
nostalgic / brings back memories /
reminds me of the good old days / reminds me of ~

不思議ですね
strange / unusual / intriguing / curious / fascinating

嫌いです（〜が嫌いです）
dont (doesnt) like / dislike / not fond of ~ / hate

くだらない
boring / lame / stupid

好みじゃない
not my cup of tea / not my interest / not my taste / not my favourite / not something i like / not something i want / not so interested

興味ある
(be 動詞) interested in ~ / (be 動詞) intrigued with ~

Useful Phrases

興味ない
(be 動詞) not interested in ~ / dont (doesnt) care about ~

おもしろい
interesting / fun / fascinating

つまらない／おもしろくない
lame / boring / dumb

感動した
i was moved (by ~) / i was touched (by ~) / ~ moved my heart / ~ touched my heart / it was emotional / it was touching / it struck me / it struck a chord in me

困った
in trouble / stuck / in a tight spot / between a rock and a hard place / trapped / having trouble

困ります
that would be troublesome / that would not work / sorry i cant / that would cause problems

寂しい
lonely / i miss you / i miss ~

寂しかった
i was lonely / it was lonely / i missed you / i missed ~

好きです（〜が好きです）
I (we, they) like ~

どうでもいい
i dont care / whatever / screw it / i dunno

めんどくさい
troublesome / tedious / pain in the neck / pain in the ass / PITA / Pain in the butt

苦手
not used to ~ / not my style / not my forte / not comfortable with ~ / not my best strength / not good at ~

不安です
worried / feeling uneasy

わけわかんない
i dont get it / it doesnt make any sense / its rubbish / its BS

Useful Phrases

減るもんじゃないし
its just a little bit of ~ / its just a little bit / its just a bite / its just a tab / its just a piece

気に入った
I (we, they) like ~ / he (she, it) likes ~ / good / nice / excellent

気になる
im curious / it bothers me / it bugs me / I wanna (want to) know / i need to know

どうしよう
What should I do?

本気です
im serious / i mean business / im not kidding / im not joking / i mean it

まいったな
thats tough / that makes it hard / this is difficult / this is a problem / i have a problem / im screwed

まじ
seriously / for real / really

20 あやまる・お詫び Apologising

ごめんなさい
sorry / im sorry / i apologise / my apologies

すみません / すみませんでした
im sorry / sorry / apologies / excuse me

申し訳ない
i am so sorry / i must apologise

すっかり忘れてた
i completely forgot / it completely slipped my mind

悪かったよ／悪い！（ごめん！）
Sorry / Sry / My bad

あやまるよ
I apologise

後悔してる
I regret it.

許して
please forgive me

Useful Phrases

そんなつもりじゃなかった
I didn't mean it.

失礼！
Excuse me.

うめあわせするよ
I'll pay you back someday. / I'll repay you're kindness.

もうしないよ
I won't do it again.

21 悪態をつく・非難・あぶない・悪い表現
Expressing anger, frustration, and disapproval

アホ
idiot / dumb ass / stupid

うざい
annoying / getting on my nerves / he(she) gets on my nerves

うっとうしい
in the way / annoying / gets in the way

うるさい
noisy / wont be quiet / wont shut up（強い表現です）

うんざりです
Im sick and tired of this / im sick of this / sick of~ / tired of~ / had enough of~ / dont want any more of~

えらそうに
haughty / cocky / full of himself (herself, themselves) / full of it

汚い
dirty / filthy / nasty

くっそ
darn it / shoot / crap / smeg

クレーム
make a complaint / complain / sue / press charges

下品
dirty / uncivilised / nasty / bad taste / distasteful / disturbing / wrong

喧嘩
quarrel / fight / argument / clash

Useful Phrases

悪口
bad mouth / talk behind ~'s back / diss

ダサい
lame / stupid / dorky / crappy

ちくしょう
dangit! / argh! / oh shoot! / doh!

なんだと？
what? / what did you say? / are you serious? / are you kidding?

ばか
dummy / stupid / idiot / git / dumbass

ばかじゃない？
what a dumbass / what an idiot

下手くそ
unskilled / untalented / bad at ~

ミスった！
crap! / shoot! / Oh no! / Doh! / oops / uh oh

22 人を表す表現 People

あいつ
that guy（男）/ that dude（男）/ that bloke（男）/ that mate（男）/ he / she

知り合い
acquaintance / someone i know

ヤンキー
hooligan / thug

ニート
NEET (Not interested in Education, Employment, Training) / Bum / Jobless

ぼっち
loner / anti-social

リア充
celebrity / ~ is very popular / social / active

イケメン
pretty boy / handsome guy / cool guy

セレブ
celebrity

23 性格・人柄を表す表現
personality and character

積極的
active / energetic / in high spirit / friendly

消極的
passive / negative / shy

神経質
nervousness / nervous（神経質な）/ nervously（神経質に）

KYだ
he (she, it) is clueless / they (we) are clueless / he (she, it) cant take a hint / they (we) cant take a hint / ~ is oblivious to his (her) surroundings / ~ is socially awkward

冷たい
cold / indifferent / aloof / heartless

恐い
scary / frightening / terrifying

あたたかい
warm / kind

やさしい
kind / nice

クール
cool

明るい
bright / happy

面白い
funny / interesting

無口
silent / not talkative

おしゃべり
talkative / chatty

24 便利な言い回し表現
Convenient expressions

意外と
Surprisingly / Unexpectedly / Interestingly

(〜に) 言っておく/伝える
ill pass it on / ill tell him(her, them) / ill let him(her, them) know / ill tell him (her, them) you said that

Useful Phrases

言っとくけど
im warning you / just for the record / just to put on record / if you ask me / if I may say something / If i may

いつも通り
as usual / as always / like before / like always before / as things always are (were)

いつものようです
his (her, its) usual self / their usual selves / nothing special / nothing unusual / as always / as usual / normally

〜くらい
about 〜 / around 〜 / somewhere around 〜 / approximately 〜 / in the ball park of 〜

実は 〜
actually 〜 / really 〜 / well 〜 /

えっと…／えーっと…
um... / let me see...

せっかくだから
while we're at it, we should 〜 / it would be a shame not to 〜 / it would be a waste not to 〜 / since 〜, why dont we 〜 / since 〜 , we should 〜

ちなみに
by the way / on that note / on a side note / speaking of which

なぜなら
because / cause / cuz

そういえば
by the way

どうぞ
go ahead / be my guest / after you / help yourself / make yourself at home / make urself comfortable

～てみる／～てみます
ill try to ~ / ill see if i can ~ / let me try to ~ / let me see if I can ~

もしかしたら
maybe / possibly / its possible that ~ / it could be that ~

万が一のために
just in case / in case we (he, she I, it, they) ~

時間をつぶす
kill time / killing time

Useful Phrases

25　他の便利ワード　other convenient phrases

食べ放題
all you can eat

オシャレ
fancy / posh（イギリス）/ nice / stylish

勘違い
mistake / error / misunderstanding

癖
habit / tendency / ~ tends (tend) to

手伝い
help out / lend a hand / give a hand / aid

普段
usually / normally / commonly

普通に
common / ordinary / usual / as always / as usual

こっそり
quietly / secretly / sneakily / in secret / privately / behind the back / without anyone knowing

絶対
absolutely / completely / utterly / no matter what / no matter the cost

徹夜
pull off an all nighter / stay up all night / party all night（遊んで）/ work all night（仕事で）

ぶらぶら
killing time / wandering around / waking around / lounging here and ther

わざと
on purpose / purposefully / intentionally

もったいない
such a waste / such a pity

珍しい
rare / uncommon / unusual

めちゃくちゃ
completely / utterly / absolutely

それぞれ
this and that / all / every / every different ~

Useful Phrases

26 携帯電話 Mobile phones

電池がない
im running low on batteries / im almost out of battery life / my battery is running low / im down to ~ percent / my battery is almost dead

電池切れ
im out of batteries / my battery is dead / im out of juice / my phone is dead

電波いい
the reception is good / im getting good reception

電波悪い
bad reception / no connection / no reception / im not getting any reception / my reception is weak / weak signal

ネットを見る
browsing the web / surfing the web

メール（SMSなど）
text / txt / message / msg

メール（SMS）して
text me / send me a msg

メールするよ（SMS）
I'll text u / I'll send you a msg.

27 さようなら Saying goodbye

さようなら
good bye / so long / bye bye / see you later / see you / c u ltr / c u / farewell

あとで
see you later / c u ltr / c u / see you

じゃあ、また連絡するね
k, ill call u / ttyl (Talk to you later)

またね／それじゃまた
see ya / c u / ltr / c ya / later / see you later

〜によろしく
say hi to 〜 for me / tell 〜 i said hi / give 〜 my (best) regards

行かなきゃ（これ以上お話できない）
Sorry I have to go / Gotta go / Sry gtg / i better get going

Useful Phrases

いってらっしゃい
see you later / have a good day / have a nice day / later!

行ってきます
see you later / see you when I get back / later!

おやすみなさい
good night / nite / night night / g'nite / sleep tight

寝ます
good night/ night night / nite nite / g'nite / im off to bed / im hitting the sack / im going to bed / im going to sleep

● 著者紹介

Nicholas Woo（ニコラス・ウー）

10年以上、日本と韓国で英語を教える。言葉と文化の関係で専門家と認められ韓国やアメリカの政府と国連で語学の専門家及び助言者として従事。2008年より日本や韓国で英語教材の開発にかかわる。現在、早稲田大学で教育とICTの研究に携わりながらGinko Laboratoryのコンテンツ・クリエーターを務めている。
[主な著書]『ネイティブならこう書くこう返すEメール英語表現』『ネイティブがネットで使っている英語』（以上ベレ出版）

翻訳アシスタント：Yuka Hashimoto
Script アシスタント：Haruka Inoue, Yusei Kikuchi, Asuka (Atchu) Kimoto, Mayu Omata, Toshiki Watanabe
Special thanks to Kazu Ishiwata, Hiro Kawano, Waka Satake, Saika Sawaki, Sunmin Kim, Nanami Kikuchi

---

英語でSNSトーク そのまま使えるネイティブ表現800

2014年 9 月25日　初版発行
2017年 4 月17日　第3刷発行

著者	Nicholas Woo
カバーデザイン	田栗克己
イラスト	いげためぐみ

ⓒ Nicholas Woo 2014, Printed in Japan

発行者	内田真介
発行・発売	ベレ出版 〒162-0832 東京都新宿区岩戸町12 レベッカビル TEL　03-5225-4790 FAX　03-5225-4795 ホームページ http://www.beret.co.jp/ 振替 00180-7-104058
印刷	三松堂株式会社
製本	根本製本株式会社

落丁本・乱丁本は小社編集部あてにお送りください。送料小社負担にてお取り替えします。

本書の無断複写は著作権法上での例外を除き禁じられています。購入者以外の第三者による本書のいかなる電子複製も一切認められておりません。

ISBN978-4-86064-407-9 C2082　　　　　編集担当　綿引ゆか